How to Think Like a

MILLIONAIRE

How to Think Like a

MILLIONAIRE

MARK FISHER
WITH MARC ALLEN

Second Edition

NEW WORLD LIBRARY
NOVATO, CALIFORNIA

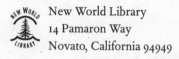 New World Library
14 Pamaron Way
Novato, California 94949

Type design by Tona Pearce Myers

Library of Congress Cataloging-in-Publication Data
Fisher, Mark.
How to think like a millionaire / Mark Fisher, with Marc Allen. — 2nd ed.
    p.   cm.
Includes bibliographical references.
ISBN 978-1-57731-643-5 (pbk. : alk. paper)
1. Success—Psychological aspects. I. Allen, Mark. II. Title.
BF637.S8F56 2008
158.1—dc22   2008015731

First printing of second edition, August 2008
ISBN 978-1-57731-643-5
Printed in Canada on 100% postconsumer-waste recycled paper

g New World Library is a proud member of the Green Press Initiative.

10 9 8 7 6 5 4 3

Contents

Editor's Preface   vii

Author's Preface   xi

Introduction   1

CHAPTER 1: Where Do I Start?   7

CHAPTER 2: Wealth Is a State of Mind   27

CHAPTER 3: Eliminating Mental Blocks   43

CHAPTER 4: Making Decisions   57

CHAPTER 5: Do What You Love   73

CHAPTER 6: The Magic of Goals   89

CHAPTER 7: A Plan of Action   101

Conclusion   111

References   115

About the Authors   119

Editor's Preface

This is a book about success cowritten by two people who have been there and are writing from their personal experience. They have taken on the challenge of summarizing as clearly and briefly as possible everything they have learned and put into practice that has contributed to their success. The results are powerful — but then, two remarkable people contributed to this book:

Mark Fisher, in his book *The Instant Millionaire*, gave us a fable-like telling of his life's story, featuring his mentor, who taught him the principles and practices necessary to becoming a financial success.

Marc Allen is the author of *Visionary Business: An Entrepreneur's Guide to Success*, a leading-edge guide for anyone in any type of business. This book is excellent for initiating change in an existing corporate culture or in setting an exciting, successful course for a new business.

The two of them together encourage all of us — and better yet, *show* all of us how — to create our own unique form of success, however we define it: whatever we dream of, whatever we wish to create in our lives.

How to Think Like a Millionaire teaches in a clear, understandable, simple way — with practical, workable procedures based on Universal Law — how to open the door to a revitalizing, life-changing way of thinking. There are nuggets of pure gold in its pages, crystal-clear recipes for success.

How to Think Like a Millionaire is not a book to be hurriedly or superficially read. It must be absorbed deeply to receive the wisdom it contains. I urge you, after reading it once or twice, to give it slow, deep, and deliberate consideration and to apply the recommended action steps at the end of each chapter in a way that fits your own nature and understanding.

I encourage you to read these pages with a mind that is open to all possibilities. Because I know, through personal experience, that if you apply the principles described in this book wisely and intelligently, there can be no uncertainty as to the outcome of any endeavor, and no limit to your success.

Becky Benenate
former editorial director
New World Library

Author's Preface

Over the years, enthusiastic readers from all over the world have written me many wonderful letters. Most of them ask me about *The Instant Millionaire*'s formula to become rich and happy.

I've tried my best to answer their questions, but I have not been able to answer all the letters in as much detail and as thoughtfully as I would like. I often thought about this problem and even meditated on it as I contemplated the heart of a Queen Elizabeth rose — my favorite! — that grows in my garden. . . .

One day, a solution came to me: I would write

one long letter that would attempt to answer all the questions I had been asked. The letter grew and grew, as I kept adding to it over a period of nearly three years. It got so long that it was too lengthy to easily duplicate — and I realized I had a book-length manuscript on my hands.

I sent it to my publisher — and friend — Marc Allen, who had just written a very impressive and inspiring book, *Visionary Business: An Entrepreneur's Guide to Success*. Marc was so enthusiastic about all my notes that he wanted not only to publish them, but to add a lot of his ideas as well. We collaborated for several months, through several drafts, and he added so much that I felt he deserved credit as a coauthor. And Becky Benenate, former editorial director of New World Library, added quite a bit as well, as a highly supportive and capable editor.

The result was exciting: Two self-made millionaires from very different backgrounds writing back and forth, attempting to summarize every valuable piece of advice we have ever received, and everything we have put into practice, into a single, concise work.

It has certainly evolved far beyond my initial idea! With every addition, every rewrite, it grew stronger and stronger, until it was something I feel honored and proud to have published. I hope you will find it a powerful and practical tool to help you truly succeed — in any and every way you choose to define success.

One can never consent to creep
when one feels an impulse to soar.

— HELEN KELLER

Introduction

Success is an attitude. Success is a habit. Success is easily available to all who want it, *believe* they can have it, and put their desires into action.

Success has no secrets. Many who achieve it readily tell their stories of devoting years to their work, to their passion and dreams, before they finally became successful. The main theme is always the same; in every case: *They love their work*. They would have done it anyway. Great fortunes — or at least some level of financial stability and success — were often part of the dream, but the wealth was a by-product of following their passion. Could you imagine Steven Spielberg making a million dollars a day if he hated movies and funny-looking extra-terrestrials? What if Henry Ford hadn't been fascinated with machinery? If Donna Karan hated clothes? When we do what we love, offering our gifts and talents, without causing harm to anyone, we are working at the highest level of service for ourselves, those around us, and our planet.

Success can't be attributed to fate, but to the deliberate application of very specific principles. Luck may be involved, but only because, as has been said, luck occurs when preparation meets opportunity.

Age, education, money, background, and childhood experience do not matter in the face of these principles. The childhoods of the world's richest self-made millionaires, successful artists, and noted performers were many times rather commonplace, often poor, and sometimes miserable. At school, many of them were considered slow learners. Yet, each one of them, at a crucial moment in their lives, decided to take their fate into their own hands and, enlightened by a book, by the word or example of another, or by a powerful sense of intuition, set out to be successful.

You may have reached that critical point that will change your life. No matter how old you are or what circumstances you may be in, all you have to do is be alert and receptive — and believe. Know that it's possible to start from scratch — as so many others have done — and achieve even your loftiest goals. It's just a matter of believing it is possible and becoming determined to create the life you desire.

In our instant-gratification society, we often look only at the final product: the movie star, the millionaire, the acclaimed artist. It looks like overnight success. We don't see the years of dedication and patient persistence that went into the process. Dustin Hoffman joked that it took him ten years to become an overnight success. And Ray Kroc, the founder of McDonald's, wrote in his autobiography, "I was an overnight success all right, but thirty years is a long, long night."

A very important aspect of successful people is that they all had failures, sometimes many failures. Most people never reach success because they give up after one or two setbacks. Napoleon Hill's classic *Think and Grow Rich* recounts the story of a miner who gave up after months of prospecting — three feet from the gold. But he applied this lesson to everything in his life thereafter and eventually became very successful.

As we begin the new millennium, success takes on a new meaning. Fewer people are interested in maintaining a workaholic fever to achieve millions while sacrificing health and home life. Success and prosperity now certainly include a balanced life: performing satisfying work while maintaining fitness and health, having loving relationships and a happy family life, being involved in social activities and causes, and having a sense of inner peace and fulfillment. In a recent *New York Times* poll, most people surveyed said it was more important to them to slow down, work less, and spend more time with friends and family than to pursue more prestige and possessions.

True success can include all of this. Presenting our passionate work to the world is a service to all those around us. Building beautiful relationships and having the time to relish them is an ambition we can all achieve, if we choose to. Well-thought-out work habits — especially the habits of mind — can bring financial security and wealth. With wealth, we have greater freedom to pursue what we enjoy, as well as to give back to the world and help others.

An old Chinese proverb says that a journey of a thousand miles begins with one step. By deciding to read this book you have just taken the first step toward success and living your dreams. Everything in life is a matter of choice. The purpose of this book is not only to help you clarify the options open to you so that you can discover what you really want, but also to help you to achieve those goals.

Perhaps, like so many others, you're unemployed, underemployed, misemployed, or otherwise dissatisfied with your present job. Despite what you may think, despite the "hard times" we are experiencing (that oft-repeated, age-old fallacy, as we shall see further on), despite unemployment and inflation, you can find the ideal job you dream of — faster than you ever believed possible. In spite of the fact that most people presume you can't always do everything you want to in life, you can find a career that will truly satisfy you. It is your right, after all. Your poverty, ill health, loneliness, and misery serve absolutely no one.

A word of warning: Quite often you'll find advice on developing entrepreneurship and setting up a business. This isn't meant to encourage you to drop everything you are doing and go into business for yourself. Not everyone is cut out for this. You need a certain type of personality, and you have to feel a real need to go out on your own. If you feel this urge, then you probably already have the basic qualities of an entrepreneur. This book can be a guide. But even if you aren't the entrepreneurial type, this book will still show you how to improve your position in life, your material assets, and your outlook, without compromising your basic security.

Some of these principles might seem original and surprising, others might seem commonplace. Don't let appearances deceive you. Success depends on them. Don't be put off by the apparent simplicity of some of these golden rules. The most obvious ideas are sometimes the most difficult to incorporate into our daily routine. Take some time to think them over. Are you applying them already? Are they part of your life and working habits?

Read this book slowly. Stop and reflect often on the words, and apply them to your life's experience. There is repetition in this book: These simple truths must be repeated, again and again, until we understand them consciously and, even more important, until the subconscious mind absorbs them and acts on them. Then we see great changes happening in our lives.

"Give me a lever and a point of support," said Archimedes, "and I will lift the world." To achieve success, you need leverage. Here, in this book, is the leverage and support for you to achieve your dreams.

Chapter One

WHERE DO I START?

The secret of getting ahead is getting started.
The secret of getting started is breaking your
complex overwhelming tasks into small manageable
tasks, and then starting on the first one.
— MARK TWAIN

Socrates, the Greek philosopher, was profoundly aware of the weakness in his own nature. Yet he came to realize that people are evolving beings, capable of changing and growing toward an ideal. People can always improve themselves. That is part of our greatness. And that ability to improve ourselves can develop at any moment in life.

BELIEVE YOU CAN BE SUCCESSFUL

You have to believe you can be successful before you will ever succeed. Sounds like a cliché, doesn't it? But take time to stop and think about it. Where else can you begin? *Your beliefs create your life experience* — it's not the other way around. And no matter what you believed before, you can change your beliefs and change your life. It's impossible to create success without believing — deeply — that you are capable of being successful. It's impossible to live abundantly without believing that you deserve abundance. Our education, society, and other forms of mental conditioning are all, unfortunately, more pessimistic than optimistic. How often has someone told you not to waste your time on pipe dreams, that you have to be realistic, that you can't have what you want? Because we hear this so often and, as a result, believe it to be true, wealth always seems reserved for the fortunate few. Success seems an exclusive party to which we are cordially not invited.

But this is simply not true. If success and prosperity are an exclusive club, it's because they are so in the minds of people whose attitudes bar their own entry. Every successful person at some point came to believe that one day he or she would be successful.

Your beliefs about success are, no doubt, deeply ingrained, and you have to be open to changing them before you'll ever succeed. Examine your beliefs to see how they have affected your life. Many people needlessly sabotage themselves because of unexamined "core beliefs" about how the world operates. Marc Allen sums it up in *Visionary Business*:

It's important — in some cases *critically* important — to regularly take time to examine our lives. The first thing to do is to take a look at our past — as clearly and honestly as we can — and discover the important events and influences that have shaped our lives. . . . Some of these shaping events have led to very good core beliefs — and those moments should be remembered, and those beliefs should be encouraged and supported. All of us have had someone in our lives who saw our potential and supported us in one way or another. We've all had glimpses of our genius, as children, and we've all had other forces that have sought to crush our genius, through doubt, through cynicism, through lack of faith.

We need to reflect on these things occasionally. Those shaping moments that have had a negative impact on us need to be looked at, and we need to discover the negative core beliefs we formed as a result. Once those beliefs are identified, they can be let go of. Because they aren't true — they're simply self-fulfilling things that become true if we believe them. This is the process of becoming conscious — becoming aware of the forces that drive us, and learning how to act on those forces, how to shape our destiny, how to become powerful. How to achieve what we want in life.

What are your beliefs about success? Don't be afraid to analyze your thoughts more closely; you may be surprised at the barriers you have put between yourself and success, once you think about it. When you realize that you can change even your most deeply held beliefs, you can come to see that not only is it possible for you to become as successful as you would like — in all areas of your life — but also that it's easy, much easier than you have ever dreamed possible. In fact, dozens of opportunities appear to you every day. Profitable ideas flash through your mind, but you usually let them slip away without pursuing them with concrete action. The art of self-suggestion, which is discussed throughout this book, helps you discover how to develop your powers of intuition — the sixth sense for success. You already have these qualities, but you may not be fully aware of their existence. You only need to access them — and you can, quite easily.

SUCCEEDING IS NO HARDER THAN FAILING

For most people, failure has become a way of life. Failure is a hard habit to break; after all, our social climate has given us high expectations, but our social conditioning has given us low morale. It's a vicious cycle. In order to become successful, we have to understand that *success is basically no more difficult than failure*. It's simply based on a different kind of mental programming, one to which the subconscious mind is not inherently opposed.

Doesn't every failure involve a highly complex combination of circumstances? Consider what it takes to miss perfect opportunities, to misfire every time you attempt something, to avoid meeting the people who can help you on your path of success, to dismiss your ideas as useless when they could lead to something worthwhile, and to continually repeat the motions that lead to defeat. It's quite an achievement to fail, and yet the subconscious mind accepts defeat as natural. Throughout this book, we analyze the vital role the subconscious plays in manifesting success. When we understand how to get the power of our subconscious mind working on success rather than failure, we will succeed. It is inevitable.

We create all sorts of excuses to block our success. How many of these thoughts creep into your mind?

• Everything was much easier in the good old days.

This excuse is proven wrong every single day of the year. While negative, shortsighted people drone on about unemployment, downsizing, and outsourcing, thousands of small businesses start and flourish every year. Thousands — globally, *millions* — of people become millionaires each year! Think of the movies produced, the books published, the new opportunities in computer science and Internet media! Think of the parts of the world that are opening to free trade! Becoming successful is not only possible today; it's actually easier than it used to be. The entire world is ours to offer our new ideas, products, services — whatever gift we have to give. Success depends far less on outside circumstances than on our mental attitude, our beliefs about ourselves and the world.

• I'm too young.

Tell this to Debbie Fields, founder and owner of Mrs. Fields Cookies, who was in her twenties when she achieved success, or Steve Jobs, founder of

Apple Computers, who made his first million when he was twenty-three, his first ten million at twenty-four, and his first hundred million at twenty-five. There is an old saying: "A youth with a single aim in life arrives early at the harvest." Youth is more often than not an asset. Lack of experience can be compensated for by boldness, daring, instinct, and originality. History shows that most successful people started out completely inexperienced and learned as they went along.

• I'm too old.

Colonel Sanders and Georgia O'Keeffe would disagree. Napoleon Hill's survey of the wealthy showed that many successful people don't reach their goals until midlife and beyond. It could be that this is the time of reaping the benefits of a series of earlier efforts, while many others are thinking of retirement. Work does not kill. Idleness, on the other hand, is often deadly; people who take early retirement often die younger than those who keep working. The fact remains that many people begin a second or third career, sometimes the most successful of all, late in life. Age is irrelevant. Your years of experience, even if you have failed, are priceless to you.

• I have no capital.

Most people don't, in the beginning. Money isn't essential when we start out. A good creative idea or business idea and a positive mental outlook are essential. Everyone in the world has at least one talent, one passion, one hobby that can become profitable if applied correctly. Contrary to popular belief, there is no shortage of money in the world. The money for launching ideas and furthering good in our world is always available.

Poverty seems to be a tradition in far too many families, an inherited trait like the color of one's hair or eyes, passed down from generation to generation. It's often more difficult for people whose families have always been poor to imagine that one day they can become rich. The image we get of ourselves and of life in general is often tinged with hopelessness and pessimism, and the role models that surround us are not always very inspiring. But there are so many exceptions to this — look at Charlie Chaplin, for example, one of history's wealthiest actors. He spent his youth in poverty, wandering the streets of London. The humiliation of poverty and early contact with life's harsh realities have in many cases spurred people on to great achievement.

• I'm not educated.

Thomas Edison left school before the age of sixteen. Microsoft's Bill Gates is a college dropout. Even though many successful people weren't educated in the formal sense, they *did* acquire an in-depth knowledge of the industry in which they made their fortunes.

• I don't have any special talent.

Many successful people displayed no early signs of being destined for fame, fortune, and fulfillment. J. Paul Getty said, "I most certainly was not a born businessman." Many people talk themselves into believing that they don't have an inborn talent or what it takes to change their lives. They go to great lengths to justify their lack of success. But in reality, everyone in the world has some talent, some kind of gift. Once we discover our own unique gift, it becomes our purpose to develop it, and doing so leads to our success.

• I don't have the energy it takes.

There is often an important difference between those who succeed and those who fail: their levels of energy. Every action we take requires a minimum amount of energy, especially mental or psychic energy. Low vitality inevitably breeds low motivation. This appears to be another inescapable vicious cycle. But all it takes is a tiny spark to ignite the resources of energy that lie dormant within us. The potential energy we all have is enormous. In many people, it is hibernating, waiting to be activated.

Yet at the same time, it takes much more energy to do something we don't like than something we enjoy. Think of the energy you have and how time slips away when you're absorbed in your favorite project. When we do what truly interests and motivates us, the energy flows easily and effortlessly.

• I'm afraid of failure.

We're born with two fears: falling and loud noises. All other fears are acquired. Unfortunately, the fear of failure is powerful and widespread — and it is paralyzing. Often deeply embedded within us, it results from past failures, from a lack of confidence bred unknowingly by our parents, and it's enforced by society's general negative, short-sighted thinking.

The fear of failure is sometimes expressed overtly but is most often unconscious and subtly disguised. People don't admit they're afraid of failing; instead, they denigrate others for building castles in the air, and they scorn dreams and creative ideas. They're champion excuse-makers: family obligations, problems, lack of time, lack of money. But wouldn't the family prefer a spouse or parent who is content with his or her work? Wouldn't time be better spent in creative expression? Wouldn't creating fulfillment resolve many problems?

Then there are the "if only" people: If only their boss would notice them. . . . If only they could come up with a good idea. . . . If only they had more talent, ability, time, money, or luck. . . . If only they had been born in different circumstances, or under another astrological sign. . . .

Obviously, if you never try anything, chances are you will never fail. But then, you're not likely to succeed either. Success doesn't miraculously appear out of the blue. It's always the result of concrete action and a positive mental attitude. Thomas Edison made hundreds — some say thousands — of attempts before perfecting the incandescent lightbulb. Abraham Lincoln lost eighteen elections before becoming president of the United States. We're not singing the praises of failure, but we know through experience that every personal defeat can be an education in itself, at least if it's accepted with an open mind.

• All I've done is fail.

One underlying reason for many people's paralyzing fear of failure is that they have already failed, or at least believe they were unsuccessful in the past. Each new setback reinforces this feeling and undermines their self-confidence. People start with one failure and see themselves as losers, and this in turn leads inevitably to more aborted attempts. These failures reinforce their loser mentality, and soon it becomes habitual. They end up believing that life is a series of hard knocks, defeats, struggles, and frustrations.

Why have you failed until now? Maybe you wanted to fail — at least on some level, possibly subconsciously. If the success you're entitled to always slips through your fingers, ask yourself why you've condemned yourself to mediocrity. And reassure yourself that even the strongest, most powerful negative programming can be changed — quickly and completely.

Once you examine it closely, you may be surprised at your inner resistance to success. You may be surprised at your negative inner monologue, which most people relentlessly repeat out of habit. Here's an important point: Your mind is always working for your welfare — it just may be working for a long outmoded goal. For instance, maybe your high energy or enthusiasm for something as a child brought harsh criticism from your parents or siblings. You very quickly learned to be quiet and restrained. But now, as an adult, there's no reason to remain unseen and unheard — yet no one told your subconscious mind.

Look at it this way: Our failures should be seen as stepping-stones that bring us closer to our goal. Our failures give us tremendous feedback. Isn't it true that with each perceived failure we learn something of value? Failure is our way of learning and growing. In reality, there is no such thing as failure: It's just part of our education on the way to our inevitable success — if we look at it that way.

Your situation will not improve if you do nothing about it. Of course, this is obvious. But then why are so many people waiting for their big break, or to win the lottery, or for some other miracle? Most people live with the idea that everything will magically work out. And then comes disappointment. Success isn't handed to us on a silver platter; we have to take action, we have to challenge our old beliefs, and we have to risk failure.

What do most people do when they need money? Some borrow, and get deeper in debt. Others tighten their belts and adapt their needs to their meager income. Instead of challenging themselves and their world to fulfill their dreams, most people limit their dreams to their perceptions of the world's constraints. They have a passive, wait-and-see attitude — "Let's see if this miracle happens." And, most often, it doesn't happen.

OUR LIVES REFLECT OUR BELIEFS — UNLIMITED SUCCESS COMES FROM AN UNLIMITED BELIEF SYSTEM

To improve your financial situation, to track down a job, to get a raise in your salary, to double your income, to become fit and healthy, you have to passionately want to improve your life. You have to take action, adopt precise measures, and change your attitude. This has to become a fixed objective. This overriding desire is mandatory to create the life you want. Determination and will are all the strength you need. Kazuo Inamori, CEO of Kyocera International and author of *A Passion for Success*, puts it this way:

> An entrepreneur must first have a clear vision of what he or she wants. A mere dream of what you want is not adequate. Instead, cultivate a desire so strong and a vision so clear that they become part of your subconscious mind.

So many people honestly desire to improve their lives but still fail in their attempts to become successful. The reason is that they have mistaken *wishing* for *wanting*. Wishful thinking is far more common than really wanting something. A wish is weak, changeable, and passive. It's not strong enough to overcome procrastination or other obstacles that may arise in the process of getting what you want. Really wanting something is a spur to action. It does not tolerate delays. It bypasses obstacles. It gives us wings to fly.

One day a wise man was asked by a disciple what it took to obtain wisdom. The sage led the disciple to a river and plunged his head underwater. After a few seconds, his anxious follower began struggling, afraid he was going to drown. But the teacher continued to hold his head underwater. The student struggled even harder. Finally, the wise man let him go just before he would have drowned and asked him, "When your head was underwater, what did you want most?" "To breathe," the frightened boy answered. "Well, there you have it. That's exactly how much you must want wisdom." And for those of us seeking to improve our lives, that's how much we must want success.

Life gives you what you sincerely want. James Allen wrote in his classic work *As You Think*, "If you cherish a vision, a lofty ideal in your heart, you will realize it. . . . You will become as great as your dominant aspiration." If you content yourself with mediocrity, that is what you will have.

Since you're reading this book, you're probably not completely satisfied with your situation. But this dissatisfaction is a gift, as there is something intensely motivating about dissatisfaction: it fuels dreams. As we mentioned before, many successful people had difficult, impoverished childhoods. They felt humiliated. Their desire to rise above poverty and low social status was so intense that it propelled them toward their dreams.

It is important to bear in mind, however, that even if you have high aspirations, you will still encounter obstacles. "Even with such strong desires, circumstances will change . . ." Inamori says. "Still, do not use these circumstances as excuses. Your determination should be so strong as to overcome any obstacles, foreseen or unforeseen."

The dreams you carry and nourish in your heart are your most noble part. Those who stop dreaming, those who ignore their most intense yearnings are living a life of emptiness and frustration. Don't let this happen to you. Change your life by daring to let yourself be carried away by your dreams and to live out your dreams to the fullest.

This philosophy may appear naive — it is.

Without naivete, without the innocence of dreams, nothing great would have been created in this world. Humans would not fly; epic films would not have been made; Ford wouldn't have created the mass-produced automobile; Edison wouldn't have lit the world. A serious outlook, cynicism, and even strictly rational thought are great obstacles to success. We aren't arguing in favor of extravagant, irrational behavior. Far from it! The truth is: At the root of every great discovery and exceptional success story lies a dream, an aspiration, a desire. This desire transcends cynicism and strictly rational thought.

Within your deepest desires and highest dreams are the keys to your success.

❧ SUMMARY AND RECOMMENDED ACTION ❧

To sum up this first chapter, there are four initial conditions to fulfill in order to become successful:

1. *Believe you will be successful.* The first prerequisite is having faith, believing that you can attain success, believing in yourself. This belief can be created by using

self-suggestion to change your old programming. If you don't believe in yourself or your ideas, you'll never convince
anyone else to believe in them. Success
never comes out of the blue, handed to
you on a silver platter. The obstacles you'll
have to overcome, the difficulties you'll
inevitably meet, and the sustained effort
you need to make all require a good dose
of faith to spur you on.

2. *Be aware that your situation will not magically change if you do nothing about it.*
Set a clear goal, and take whatever steps
you can each week to move a little closer
to the goal. Great success is the result of
a great many small steps. It doesn't require taking huge, scary leaps; it only requires taking the next obvious step in
front of you.

3. *Passionately desire to improve your life.*
Make a list of the excuses and the inner
monologues that keep success at bay.
This stage is absolutely essential. It makes
you aware of your limiting beliefs. Once
you know them, you can overcome them.

Successful people have learned to release doubt from their minds. They have tremendous faith in both themselves and in their plans, despite any opposition they may face.

4. *Dare to dream — and to dream great dreams.* Within your deepest desires and highest dreams are the keys to success. Your subconscious mind knows only those limitations you have imposed upon it through your own limiting beliefs — and those beliefs can be changed, using the tools in this book.

Chapter Two

WEALTH IS
A STATE OF MIND

Mind is the master power that molds and makes,
And we are mind, and evermore we take
The tool of thought, and shaping what we will,
Bring forth a thousand joys, a thousand ills.
We think in secret, and it comes to pass,
Our world is but our looking glass.

— JAMES ALLEN, AUTHOR OF *AS YOU THINK*

The most common mistake we make is looking outside ourselves for what we can only find inside. Success is no exception. Just as the source of true happiness lies within each of us, success also comes from within. Success is the result of a very specific mental attitude. Call it what you like: the mentality of the rich, an attitude of success, prosperity consciousness. Success is the outward manifestation of an inner focus, the result of steering thoughts toward a specific target.

Unfortunately, most people are unaware of this. Most of the principles in the following chapters lead to a higher, universal truth: *The mind is capable of anything*. Genuine wealth is, above all, a state of mind — a state that has taken form in the lives of the rich and successful. We have to begin by being rich in mind before we can become rich in life, successful in mind before we can be successful in life.

Gaining a clear understanding of the subconscious is fundamental. It's all very well to tell people that they must believe in success and fortune and want it passionately. Yet, most people are paralyzed by bad experiences. They appear completely incapable of cultivating what Friedrich Nietzsche called "the will to power." It's not at all easy to demand action and firmness from someone who is uncertain, indecisive, passive, and unmotivated. By discovering the mechanisms and power of the subconscious mind, however, anyone can overcome these obstacles.

OUR SUBCONSCIOUS MIND IS LIMITLESS

We are the creators of our own happiness or misery. Truly understanding this statement can be our most important motivator.

The key to success ultimately lies in the proper use of the subconscious mind. Both the means to make money and the outside circumstances affecting us are so varied and so personal that it would be impossible to propose a single surefire winning formula to create success. No miracle recipe exists — but there is a common theme through all success stories. This single, simple theme is *a positive inner attitude*.

Analysis and research only go so far. And then our sixth sense, what some people call business sense or intuition, comes into play — the result of positive mental programming and a well-utilized subconscious mind. The subconscious mind is best represented by the image of the iceberg: The small, visible part is the conscious mind while the submerged and much larger part is the subconscious. The role of the subconscious in our lives is much greater than most of us understand. It's the seat of our habits, complexes, and the limitations of our personalities. No matter what we think, *the subconscious — not outside circumstances — is responsible for an individual's success or failure*.

There are many ways we train our subconscious. One of the strongest ways is through our beliefs. Peter Senge, author of *The Fifth Discipline*, writes:

Most of us hold one of two contradictory beliefs that limit our ability to create what we really want. The more common is the belief in our *powerlessness* — our inability to bring into being all the things we really care about. The other belief centers on *unworthiness* — that we do not deserve to have what we truly want. . . .

There are many ways by which the subconscious gets programmed. Cultures program the subconscious. Beliefs program the subconscious. It is well established, for example, that beliefs affect perception: If you believe that people are untrustworthy, you will continually "see" double-dealing and chicanery that others without this belief would not see.

The subconscious can be compared to a computer. It blindly and infallibly executes the program fed into it. An appropriate term from the computer industry is GIGO — Garbage In, Garbage Out. Much of our programming from infancy onward has been negative garbage, coming straight from negative belief systems.

In early childhood, our critical sense is still undeveloped, and we naturally accept all suggestions from the outside world. The program's database, so to speak, comes at first from parents and teachers, media and peers. Their words become engraved in our young minds, which are as impressionable as soft clay. A single word can blight someone's life, or at least weigh them down for a long time. This word may have been said without malice, but if it contained fear and negativity, the effects can be disastrous. A pessimistic mother, one day snapping in frustration, may tell a child she considers too impulsive or whimsical, "Quit dreaming — stop living in the clouds. Who do you think you are?" These remarks are recorded in the child's subconscious and become part of his or her mental programming. The job of the subconscious, which has almost limitless power, is to execute this program, making the child fail over and over again. The most tragic thing of all is that people who have had this type of early conditioning can spend their entire lives unaware that they are the victims of negative mental programming.

Words are extremely powerful agents. A declaration of love, a piece of bad news, a word of congratulations all have a major impact on our inner state. And *the words don't even have to be true for the mind to accept them.*

Thomas Peters and Robert Waterman, authors of *In Search of Excellence*, describe an experiment that illustrates the power of words, even when those words are untrue:

The old adage is "nothing succeeds like success." It turns out to have a sound scientific basis. Researchers studying motivation find that the prime factor is simply the self-perception among motivated subjects that they are, in fact, doing well. Whether they are or not by any absolute standard doesn't seem to matter much. In one experiment, adults were given ten puzzles to solve. All ten were exactly the same for all subjects. They worked on them, turned them in, and were given the results at the end. Now, in fact, the results they were given were fictitious. Half of the exam takers were told that they had done well, with seven out of ten correct. The other half were told they had done poorly, with seven out of ten wrong. Then all were given another ten puzzles (the same for each person). The half who had been *told* that they had done well in the first round really did do better in the second, and the other half really did do worse. Mere association with past personal success apparently leads to more persistence, higher motivation, or something that makes us do better.

The result of this experiment is worth some thought. The subjects' subconscious minds were influenced by the falsified results. Perception alone radically improved one group's performance and weakened the other's.

A little further on, the same authors advance the following theory as a result of this experiment: "We often argue that the excellent companies are the way they are because they are organized to obtain extraordinary effort from ordinary human beings." What applies to businesses certainly applies equally to individuals. Their secret: a well-guided subconscious mind.

In addition to parents, teachers, and friends who clumsily express negativity without realizing the harmful impact they have, there is another very important programming agent as well: the individual. All of us have our own inner monologues that program us constantly. We repeat to ourselves: "Nothing ever works out for me." "I'm always tired." "What am I doing with my life?" "I'm not appreciated enough." "I'm not good enough." "It's so hard to succeed." "I never have enough time." "I've wasted so much time." The list is endless. These negative, pessimistic thoughts that we repeat to ourselves, more or less consciously, influence or reinforce the current program.

But they don't have to stay in our consciousness. When we reach adulthood, we can take responsibility for our own belief systems. No programming has to be permanent. Any negative programming can be turned around. How? Through the power of even a single affirmation that effectively counter-acts that negative programming.

THE POWER OF AFFIRMATIONS, THE POWER OF SELF-SUGGESTION

How can we acquire a mentality that will produce favorable circumstances and attract success? There are a wide variety of methods available, all based on some form of self-suggestion. These methods have a number of different names — mental program-ming, positive thinking, affirmation, self-hypnosis, psycho-cybernetics, the Alpha method. All of these techniques have proven to be effective. Both au-thors of this book have experienced wonderful re-sults by using a simple formula, or affirmation, developed by a famous French pharmacist, Emile Coué.

Coué's discovery was accidental. One day, one of his clients insisted on buying a drug for which he needed a prescription. He had no prescription, but still stubbornly demanded the drug. Coué thought up a trick: He recommended a product that he said was just as effective, but was actually only a sugar pill. The patient came back a few days later, completely cured and absolutely delighted with the results. What was later called the placebo effect had just been discovered.

What had happened to this patient? It was essentially the same phenomenon that had occurred in the experiment in *In Search of Excellence*, except that the magical effect of words, of confidence, and of the subconscious had acted on the physical rather than the intellectual level. This patient was cured by his confidence in the pharmacist and in the medication, as well as by the mental certainty that he was going to get well.

It didn't take Coué long to realize the significance of this experiment. If a word could cure an ailment, what could it do to someone's personality? In the next few years he developed an extremely simple formula, one that involved no sugar pills — simply words. It has been applied throughout the world and has improved the lives of thousands of individuals. The formula is actually a simple self-suggestion. Since Coué couldn't stay at all of his patients' bedsides, or stay in contact with them, the patients could cure themselves using the formula, which consisted of these words: *Every day, in every way, I am getting better and better.*

Coué advised people to repeat this sentence aloud in a monotone voice at least twenty times a day. Countless variations on the formula have been conceived. We can each concoct our own according to our needs and personality. The effects are astounding. This general formula, this simple affirmation, embraces all aspects of our lives and has limitless possibilities.

The golden rule of self-suggestion is repetition, so this should be repeated daily — throughout the day — to have the best effect. A relaxed state, where the subconscious is most receptive to new information, is the best — though not essential. It makes the process effective much more quickly, however. You are naturally in a relaxed state after meditation, upon awakening, or at bedtime. Or relaxation can easily be self-induced: To do this, lie down or seat yourself comfortably in an armchair, and close your eyes. Inhale deeply several times. Then relax each separate part of the body, beginning with the feet, ankles, legs, and on up to the head.

You must literally flood your subconscious with your new formula. Little by little, a new program will set in, and a new personality will emerge. Negative reinforcement will give way to positive reinforcement, to enthusiasm, energy, boldness, and determination. Don't be put off by the simplicity of this method, as were many of Coué's contemporaries, who refused to believe that such a simple technique could be effective. As the authors of this book, we're living proof this technique is effective!

Try it, several times a day for at least a month, and see the results for yourself.

Many successful people, when faced with adversity, have subconsciously resorted to this technique or others like it. Whether confronted by problems or on the threshold of a new adventure, they learned to condition or reprogram themselves by repeating the ideas that they would reach success, that no obstacle would hinder their attempts, that their visions would certainly become reality.

The cumulative result of all our inner programming is our self-image. Despite our conscious efforts to create a self-image, each of us has only a vague idea of the one we actually project. We have an even more vague idea of the role self-image plays in our lives. It's important to understand this because people are what they believe themselves to be. Everything in our lives, including our wealth, joy, and physical shape, is directly proportional to our self-image, directly influenced by our self-image.

Peter Senge adds another important point:

Ultimately, what matters most in developing the subconscious...is the genuine caring for the desired outcome, the deep feeling of it being the "right" goal toward which to aspire. The subconscious seems especially receptive to goals in line with our deeper aspiration and values. According to some spiritual disciplines, this is because these deeper aspirations input directly to, or are part of, the subconscious mind.

His words are worth pondering.

PICTURE YOUR SUCCESS — IMAGINE IT CLEARLY

What do you want? What does your version of success look like? You are unique; you have a unique definition of success, and success can only come through your unique vision. Those who see themselves as nothing but lowly employees, who can't imagine ever being able to scale the corporate ladder, will stay in lowly positions. "There's no way I can double my income in a year!" If this is what we believe, life proves us right.

We always establish our goals according to our self-image. It's therefore just as hard for us to fail as to succeed. And it's just as easy for us to succeed as it is to fail. *A new self-image produces a new goal, and a new goal results in a new life.*

In her powerful book *Creative Visualization*, Shakti Gawain writes, "Creative visualization is the technique of using your imagination to create what you want in your life." All successful people pictured themselves successful before achieving their dreams. No matter how poor they were in the beginning, no matter how little education they had, no matter how few contacts they had, all of them pictured themselves successful. They became convinced they would be successful. Life answered their dreams in accordance with their self-image and the faith they had in their success.

Because of this direct correlation between your self-image and what life offers you, it's extremely worthwhile to work on your self-image, so that *every day in every way, you are getting better and better*. This affirmation does wonders for your self-image. You can change your self-image at any time, according to your aspirations.

In the beginning, when you start reprogramming yourself and shaping a new self-image, you'll inevitably be influenced by your old image. This is completely natural. Change takes place in gradual stages. But you'll eventually develop a new self-image, and it will produce new goals — and new goals will, inevitably, change your life for the better.

Experience has shown that to be fully effective self-suggestions or affirmations should be: (1) *brief* — if they are too long, they will not be effective — and (2) *positive*, which is absolutely essential. The subconscious works differently from the conscious mind. If you say, "I'm not poor anymore," the word *poor* might be subconsciously retained because it is the key word. Repeating the statement with the negative word could produce the opposite results of what you want. You have to take a positive, yet gradual, approach. Some authors write that you must formulate your suggestions as if you already have what you desire: "I am now rich." This *could* be counterproductive in some cases, however, because your conscious mind might see a contradiction here. Mental conflict could arise to compromise the positive results of the suggestion. If you repeat, "I am now rich," or "My job is perfect," at least some part of your mind will naturally sense the inconsistency, especially if you're broke or out of work. In our opinion, it's better to say, "I'm getting more and more successful, day by day," or "I am creating a perfect job." It's important to find the affirmation that feels positive and empowering for you.

Affirmations guarantee success. We know this from experience. Even starting with a mechanical and barely convincing repetition of your words has some effect. The more emotion and feeling you put into your suggestion, however, the better the results will be. Don't impose limitations on your affirmations. Your potential is extraordinary. As Ray Kroc, the founder of McDonald's, said, "Think big and you'll become big."

❧ SUMMARY AND RECOMMENDED ACTION ❧

To sum up this chapter, these are the ways to imprint powerful change in your life:

1. *Write down your version of success in the form of an affirmation that is particularly powerful for you.* An example might be, "I now have an annual income of $_____" or "I am creating the perfect job for myself." This simple act will have a great impact on you, giving your thoughts more power and authority. It becomes a springboard for change. Never lose sight of your affirmation — it is your formula for success. Leave it in a place where you will see it regularly, and continue to affirm it regularly.

2. *Another way to imprint powerful change is to repeat single words frequently.* For example, many successful people share the following characteristics — they are:

- Persistent
- Enthusiastic
- Energetic
- Confident
- Imaginative
- Diligent

- Bold
- Intuitive
- Persuasive
- Authoritative
- Fun-loving
- Positive
- Astute
- Dependable
- Daring
- Relaxed

Pick a word that describes a characteristic you want to strengthen in yourself, and repeat the word throughout the day. Or affirm, "I am _____." This is a very effective technique.

3. *Make a list of the qualities you would like to develop more fully, using or adding to the list above.* Choose the qualities you need to work on the most. Work on one at a time, starting with your weakest. Feel how much stronger you soon become.

4. *Affirm to yourself, repeatedly: Every day, in every way, I am getting better and better.*

Chapter Three

ELIMINATING
MENTAL BLOCKS

To succeed, we must have a desire so strong
that it reaches and permeates our subconscious minds.

— KAZUO INAMORI, FOUNDER AND CHAIRMAN
OF TWO OF JAPAN'S MOST SUCCESSFUL COMPANIES
AND AUTHOR OF *A PASSION FOR SUCCESS*

Perhaps this is the only piece of advice you'll need to create the success you want: *To succeed, we must have a desire so strong that it permeates our subconscious minds*. Once this happens, we connect with the infinite organizing power of the universe, and it supports our desire. Once this happens, we create what we want in life, and we create a new self-image in the process.

Creating a new self-image inevitably entails letting go of the old one. Yet everyone resists this kind of change. Everyone has created mental blocks that work to prevent change, even change for the good.

Mental blocks are unconscious beliefs that have been reinforced by experiences in our lives. Willis Harman discusses unconscious beliefs in his book *Global Mind Change*:

> A person's total belief system is an organization of beliefs and expectancies that the person accepts as true of the world he or she lives in — verbal and nonverbal, implicit and explicit, conscious and unconscious.
>
> The belief system does not have to be logically consistent; indeed, it probably never is.

One of the most common, deeply embedded, and harmful mental blocks is the belief that money is bad. This can often be traced to the Judeo-Christian Bible passage, "Money is the root of all evil." Actually, the entire passage reads, "The love of money is the root of all evil." Certainly, the *love* of money can promote greed and selfishness. The danger lies in becoming a slave to money — it is an excellent servant, but a cunning and powerful master. It can be seductive, drawing all one's time and energy into its acquisition. It's important to keep this in mind as you begin to make more of it — as you inevitably will if you continue reading books like this one and absorbing these principles of wealth, consciously and subconsciously. If we're honest with ourselves, we intuitively know whether our relationship with money is positive or not.

Money is badly maligned in many areas of our society, and some of the reasons are justified. But performing our service effectively — and being well rewarded for it — can be very positive, for ourselves and our world.

CREATE A POSITIVE VIEW OF MONEY — MONEY CAN BE A POWERFUL AGENT OF GOOD IN THE WORLD

Through our work we create ideas, innovative products, jobs, beautiful works of art, educational tools, and so on, endlessly. And those who truly understand real success give back to their communities and their world through philanthropy and many other forms of financial and visionary support. There are literally millions of wealthy people who are the opposite of the unscrupulous, mean-spirited money-grubber who seeks materialism for its own sake, for greedy acquisition and consumption. It's no coincidence that the richest countries in the world have also reached the highest achievements in culture and science. Money affords us the time and resources to pursue desires beyond basic human needs, to create things that are as important as survival itself.

Money is simply a recognition of services rendered. Most people who become wealthy have provided services to many people and have been justly rewarded for them. Walt Disney brightened the lives of millions of children, and adults as well. The list of contributions made by the wealthy is endless, for money is power — power to do a great deal of good in the world.

Henry Ford was once asked what he would do if he lost his entire fortune. Without a moment's hesitation, he said he would think up another fundamental human need and meet it by offering a cheaper and more efficient service than anybody else. He said that he would be a millionaire again within five years.

Many people have an aversion to money. This aversion is often hypocritical: People malign the rich but secretly envy them. Once you begin to understand some of the principles in this book and begin providing the kind of services to humanity that will make you substantial amounts of money, your attitude toward the rich will change completely — because you'll become one of them. And you'll be able to do a lot of good for a lot of people with your wealth.

Another prevalent mental block is the fear of going against family background and upbringing — outdoing one's parents, for example. Not everyone suffers from this, of course; we have already seen that poverty can be a strong catalyst for success. But in many cases, poverty is a form of neurotic behavior — a mental rut that goes nowhere, the reflection of an impoverished self-image. Mental blocks around the issue of making money come disguised in a great variety of forms that we need to examine as we recognize them in ourselves.

It's important to integrate a positive view of money and success into your new self-image. Be vigilant and honest with yourself; identify your mental blocks and release them. Identify your limiting beliefs and change them. Replace them with more positive, powerful thoughts. *Both poverty and riches are the offspring of thought.*

THERE ARE NO LIMITATIONS TO THE MIND

This is a very powerful truth, one that bears repeating: *There are no limitations to the mind except those we accept.* Once we understand this as a truth, we can become successful and shape our present and future life to match our aspirations. When we apply this truth to our lives, our circumstances become whatever we desire; our lives become whatever we want them to be.

If you steer your thoughts in a positive, expansive direction, you'll become as powerful as you can imagine. Every day, make sure that you devote some time to reprogramming yourself, to creative visualization, guided imagery, daydreaming. Many people are paid extraordinary salaries to daydream! Our most lucrative thoughts can come through daydreaming, free-rambling fantasy, and brainstorming future possibilities.

Daydreams are often maligned by "down-to-earth" people who say that we have to look life squarely in the face and accept our fate, even if it leaves a lot to be desired. Yet, these resigned and unhappy individuals forget that there are two types of dreamers: those who make no attempt to turn their dreams into reality, and those who understand and believe in the creative power of the subconscious. These are the dreamers who take concrete measures to fulfill their dreams. These are the dreamers who shape our world and who create wealth for themselves and others in the process.

In *The Seven Spiritual Laws of Success*, Deepak Chopra says:

Inherent in every intention and desire is the mechanics for its fulfillment. Intention and desire in the field of pure potentiality have infinite organizing power. And when we introduce an intention in the fertile ground of pure potentiality, we put this infinite organizing power to work for us.

Let's examine what Chopra is saying. If intention is thought and our thoughts are filled with negative ideas toward money (we can only make enough to get by, for example, or there is never enough), we will fulfill these thoughts. If, however, we fill our mind with new and positive images (there are no limits, as the universe contains infinite possibilities), we will fulfill these thoughts, and become as successful as we can possibly imagine.

Clearly imagine that you already have what you hope for, that you have reached your goals. What does your life look like? One reason this exercise of imagination is so effective is that the subconscious is not governed by the same rules of time as the conscious mind. In fact, time doesn't exist in the subconscious mind — or in our dreams, which are the subconscious mind's most easily recognizable by-product.

This is why trauma experienced in early childhood can affect people long after they are adults; rational minds understand that they no longer have to worry about the past, but the subconscious may not recognize the difference. This is also why we can pretend that something is true in our fantasies and our visualizations, and the subconscious mind will go about its work and bring what we imagine into reality, whether the things we imagine are our fears or our ardent desires for the very best.

This may seem to contradict what we said earlier (on page 40) about affirmations. In our fantasies and visualizations, however, it is very effective to imagine as fully as possible that we have created the future we dream of.

OUR THOUGHTS MATERIALIZE

All of our thoughts tend to materialize in our lives when they are repeated enough. This is why, in order to succeed, we have to monitor our thoughts closely. If we continually focus on financial troubles, we invite them to stay. *Wherever you focus your attention, wherever you put your energy, that is what will grow.* If you focus on the good that you want, you welcome abundance, prosperity, and success. If you focus on how little money you bring home every month, you will continue to experience frustration and need. However, if you focus on putting even a small amount away — just ten dollars a week in a savings account, for example — and imagine the account growing, you will begin to create abundance in your life because your focus will shift from "lack of " to "growth." Try it, and you'll be amazed at how different it feels to focus on growth rather than lack, on prosperity rather than poverty. The subconscious is a vast field, governed by the universal law of cause and effect. As we sow, so we reap. Thoughts and ideas are the cause; facts and events are the effect.

Most people have more imagination for conjuring up problems that prevent them from realizing their dreams than for recognizing their opportunities for success. Stephen Covey, author of *The Seven Habits of Highly Effective People*, emphasizes this point:

Habits have tremendous gravity pull. Like any natural force, gravity pull can work with us or against us. The gravity pull of some of our habits may currently be keeping us from going where we want to go. Breaking deeply imbedded habitual tendencies such as procrastination, impatience, criticalness, or selfishness that violate basic principles of human effectiveness involves more than a little willpower and a few minor changes in our lives. It takes tremendous effort to break free from the gravity pull of such habits, but once we do, our freedom takes on a whole new dimension.

Change — real change — comes from the inside out. . . . It comes from striking at the root — the fabric of our thought, the fundamental, essential paradigms, which give definition to our character and create the lens through which we see the world.

Successful people are inspired by their dreams, and they focus on the means to reach them, not on what's keeping them from realizing them. Inventors see their inventions. Artists see their completed works. Successful entrepreneurs see their businesses thriving. Visionaries, social workers, nonprofit workers, and even some politicians see society changed for the better.

Ted Turner, creator of a broadcast empire, said, "A visionary is supposed to have a vision of the future." Ideas govern the world. The power they have is phenomenal. It is therefore necessary to *repeatedly* fill our minds with thoughts of service, abundance, and success — to break free of the gravity pull of our negative thoughts. Eventually, we replace the old, negative thoughts with a new, positive self-image. Each thought has energy and, through some mysterious law of attraction, draws objects, beings, and circumstances of a similar nature to it — like a magnet. Negative thoughts attract negative experiences. Positive thoughts attract positive experiences.

Unfortunately, this truth is not always supported by society. Our educational system generally supports and encourages the rational and strictly logical part of thought, while neglecting or even scorning its intuitive and imaginative side. The right side of the brain is too often ignored.

And yet nothing great has ever been achieved without an original dream. A dream is a kind of projection of our inner selves. What, in fact, is a projection or a project? By definition, it's something that we throw forward. We project even our own self-images, and this projection in turn programs our minds to create success or failure depending on the quality of the projection. The greater we program our self-images to be, the more expansive our dreams will be. And our dreams, however bold, are often more easily attainable than we might even believe at the time that we form them.

Steven Spielberg once dreamed of making a certain film. He had the script, but he needed a producer to finance it. One day, while walking on the beach, he "accidentally" met a rich man who was

ready to invest in young filmmakers. With the
money Spielberg received from this producer, a
total stranger to him at the time, he was able to
shoot *Amblin*, which was given an Honorable Men-
tion at the Venice Film Festival and drew attention
to him in Hollywood.

This is often how the subconscious solves a
problem: We have a chance encounter, or we happen to see an article or TV show that provides a
clear-cut answer to a dilemma, or our family or
friends somehow contribute to our success — sometimes in ways they aren't even aware of at the time.

When others point to fate, or to difficult circumstances, believing we need to be "resigned to
our fate," we point out that the world is governed
mentally and physically by cause and effect, and so
we create our fate; it's the result of our thoughts and
actions. The same is true for good and bad luck:
They're the consequences of our thoughts and actions. We literally make our own good and bad luck.
This is why people who correctly learn and apply
the laws of the mind and success forge their own
destiny.

The supreme secret of success is a secret not because
anyone is trying to keep it secret but only because so
few understand it. This secret can be told in a few
simple words, and success will come to you when

you truly understand these words: The human mind can accomplish whatever it believes in.

Henry Ford summed it up very well in his now-famous quote: "Whether you think you can or you think you can't, you're right."

❧ **SUMMARY AND RECOMMENDED ACTION** ❧

To integrate a positive view of money and success in your life:

1. *Identify your mental blocks about money and success.* Explore your relationship with money — is it positive or negative? As you become aware of your thoughts in relation to money, write them down. Take a look at why you might have particular thoughts or beliefs. Then release any old ways of thinking that aren't supportive of your greatest dreams.

2. *Monitor your thoughts closely. Focus on the good you want.* Welcome abundance, prosperity, and success into your life. Perhaps you'll want to open a bank account, and start by putting a small amount each week into it. Whenever

your thoughts are focused on how little you have, make a conscious effort to think about your new account and its inevitable growth over the years, as you continue to add to it. You'll start to feel the difference between focusing on "growth and abundance" and focusing on "lack." Eventually your focus will shift without conscious effort. All your thoughts can be shifted this way.

3. *Reprogram your thoughts. Do some of the exercises in this book.* Every day, make sure that you devote some time to reprogramming yourself, to creative visualization, guided imagery, and daydreaming. In a relaxed state, fill your mind with new and positive images. Fantasize that you have already achieved the greatest success you can imagine. Visualize and feel what it's like to already have reached your goals. Do so *repeatedly*, day after day, week after week. You'll soon see some exciting changes happening in your life.

Chapter Four

MAKING DECISIONS

One of our greatest gifts is our intuition. It's a sixth sense we all have — we just need to learn to access it, to tap into it, and to trust it.

— DONNA KARAN, DESIGNER AND FOUNDER
OF THE INTERNATIONAL FASHION EMPIRE DKNY

Having a dream, and having confidence in yourself, is one thing — but how do you know whether your dream is a good idea, and you're not making a disastrous mistake? We are constantly called upon to make decisions, whether to look for a new job, choose a career, back a project, or make an investment.

A wrong move in business or your career, while certainly not fatal, can mean a substantial setback.

We have to learn how to make right decisions more often than wrong ones. It's encouraging to note that most successful people believe not that this ability is inborn but that it can be acquired and enhanced. This ability is accessible to anyone who takes the time and energy to cultivate it.

Of course, some plans are simply not viable. Mark McCormack, author of *What They Don't Teach You at Harvard Business School*, supplies an amusing example of this principle:

> A dog-food company was holding its annual sales convention. During the course of the convention the president of the company listened patiently as his advertising director introduced a point-of-sale scheme that would "revolutionize the industry," and his sales director extolled the virtues of the "best damn sales force in the business." Finally it was time for the president to go to the podium and make his closing remarks.
>
> "Over the past few days," he began, "we've heard from all our division heads of their wonderful plans for the coming year. Now as we draw to a close, I have only one question. If we have the best advertising, the best marketing, the best sales force, how

come we sell less damn dog food than anyone in the business?"

Absolute silence filled the convention hall. Finally, after what seemed like forever, a small voice answered from the back of the room: "Because the dogs hate it."

The best marketing in the world won't help an inferior product, or a service that doesn't fill a need. How do we know if our plan is viable or not? We've got to learn to access, tap into, and trust our intuition.

While the Wright brothers were inventing their plane, scientific studies were undertaken to demonstrate that a body heavier than air could not possibly fly. And Ray Kroc's friends thought entering the business of selling cheap hamburgers was sheer lunacy. We need to enhance our capacity to see possibilities where others see only difficulties, or even impossibilities. Sam Walton, founder and chairman of Wal-Mart, explains in his book *Sam Walton — Made in America* how recognizing opportunity out of necessity helped him make his company the phenomenal success that it is today:

Many of our best opportunities were created out of necessity. The things that we were forced to do, because we started out under-financed and undercapitalized in remote, small communities, contributed mightily to the way we've grown as a company.

Because Walton had the capacity to see possibilities where others saw only difficulties or impossibilities, his company grew and continues to grow and flourish.

This is another key to success, and it's worth giving some thought.

LOOK FOR POSSIBILITIES WHERE OTHERS SEE ONLY DIFFICULTIES

One day, over fifty years ago, a man was taking a photograph of his young daughter, and she asked him why they had to wait to see the pictures. This naive question intrigued her father, inventor Edwin H. Land. All of Land's scientist friends told him his dream was impossible and his plan a waste of time and money. In November 1948, the first 60-second Polaroid camera went on sale in Boston, and it caused a stampede of customers.

How often have you seen people raise their eyebrows at one of your seemingly impossible schemes? How often have you judged something unlikely or impossible to achieve before realizing that just the opposite was true? Because of "rational reasons," or, more often, a secret lack of confidence, we give up our dreams and console ourselves with the thought that it wouldn't have worked out anyway. This problem is directly linked with our self-image. The better our self-image, the more likely we'll be able to see that a range of possibilities exists, and the more likely we'll take the risks necessary to act on the opportunities we see.

Many unrealized plans and ideas are initially neither feasible nor unfeasible. What determines success or failure when putting them into action is the quantity and quality of the energy invested. They come to life and become viable through the sheer force of the vitality and energy put into them. People with positive, healthy self-images are powerhouses of energy and can easily tap into the unlimited reserves of their subconscious minds. They can create dog food that dogs love.

One flaw in many people who hesitate in carrying out a plan is that they try to identify all the potential obstacles they might face, and they ignore the tools they have at their disposal to combat those problems — a paralyzing, anxiety-producing attitude if ever there was one! A far more skillful and effective approach is to focus on all the reasons we're likely to succeed instead of conjuring up all the possible stumbling blocks. We must, of course, weigh pros and cons. What happens in many cases, however, is despite ten favorable reasons, one negative reason discourages most people from trying at all. This comes from our negative programming, which, through the principle of attraction, provides fertile ground for a single obstacle to thrive. Focusing on the negative can distort our judgment and paralyze our actions.

Naturally, it's extremely important to learn as much as possible beforehand about a proposed plan, job offer, or business deal. But there are always imponderables. Even the most detailed and sophisticated analysis will never completely dispel the unknown. Studies undertaken by corporations and individuals alike often simply confirm their original ideas. Facts can't take the place of intuition. We must discover how to interpret facts and draw our own conclusions from the data, using our intuition to guide us.

TRUST YOUR INTUITION

The ability to trust and rely on your sixth sense — your intuition — is the cornerstone of success. This sense can be developed so that it becomes second nature and enables you to make faster and more reliable decisions. If a plan is intuitively right for you, it excites you, it "feels good." If your plan doesn't fire you up, it's best to discard it for another — one that you believe in, one that excites you.

It's time to reeducate your intellect to recognize your intuition as a valid source of information and guidance. You can train your intellect to listen to and express your intuitive voice. The intellect is by nature very disciplined. This discipline can help you to ask for and receive the direction of your intuitive self.

How do you know when to make a decision? How do you know whether you have examined the situation enough and have all the necessary facts at your disposal? The answer is to rely on your subconscious program by repeating, "The right answer will come to me, easily and effortlessly." Or, "My inner guidance is giving me the right answer." Or, "My inner powers allow me to make the right decision." Find the words that feel best to you. With these kinds of affirmations, you are literally calling forth the wisdom of your intuitive mind.

Shakti Gawain, in *Living in the Light*, outlines a simple method of learning to trust your intuition:

What does it mean to trust your intuition?
...It means tuning in to your "gut feelings" about things — that deepest inner sense of

personal truth — in any given situation, and acting on them, moment by moment. Sometimes these "gut messages" may tell you to do something unexpected or inconsistent with your previous plans; they may require that you trust a hunch that seems illogical; you may feel more emotionally vulnerable than you are used to; you may express thoughts, feelings, or opinions foreign to your usual beliefs; perhaps follow a dream or fantasy; or take some degree of financial risk to do something that feels important to you....

How do you do it? ... Learning to trust your intuition is an art form, and like all other art forms, it takes practice to perfect. Your intuition is always 100 percent correct, but it takes time to learn to hear it correctly.

It is often hard to distinguish the "voice" of our intuition from the many other "voices" that speak to us from within: the voice of our conscience, voices of our old programming and beliefs, other people's opinions, fears and doubts, rational head trips, and "good ideas."

Unfortunately, there is no surefire way to differentiate the true voice or feelings of your intuition from all the other voices. The first step is to pay attention to what you feel inside, to the inner dialogue that goes on within you. For example, you might feel, "I'd like to give Jim a call." Immediately, the doubting voice inside says, "Why call him at this time of day? He probably won't be home," and you automatically ignore your original impulse to call. What if you had called him? What if you had found him at home, and discovered he had something important to say to you?

As you become aware of the subtle inner dialogue between your intuition and your other inner voices, it's very important not to put yourself down or diminish the experience. Try to remain an objective observer. Notice what happens when you follow your intuitive feelings. The result is usually increased energy and power, and a sense of things flowing. Now, notice what happens when you doubt, suppress, or go against your feelings. Invariably, you will observe decreased energy, powerless or helpless feelings, and emotional and/or physical pain.

Here's another effective method to use when faced with a decision to make: Toss a coin. You might think we're joking, but we're not: Flipping a coin is a time-honored little trick that can help you contact your subconscious mind. Decide what each side represents, and then flip a coin. Watch your reactions. If it lands on heads, telling you to go ahead with your plan, and you're disappointed, it's probably because you don't really believe in it or wish to pursue it. If tails appears, and you are disappointed, then maybe you should forge ahead. But if you're happy with the outcome, you have your answer. The idea is not to consider the results as definite, but to use them as a means of helping with the decision — helping you see intuitively which side you really favor.

As you learn to live from your intuition, you give up making decisions with your head. You act moment by moment on what you feel, and you allow things to unfold as you go. In this way, you are led in the right direction. Decisions are made easily and naturally.

If you're having difficulty making a decision, take a break. The break could last a minute, an hour, or a day or more. Allow time to review the facts, then set a deadline: "At 3:00 PM I will tell the Board my decision." The time frame will activate your intuitive decision-making process.

Another time-honored solution is to sleep on the problem. "Sleep is the mother of counsel." This old adage is true because we easily contact our subconscious at night. So many problems that seemed so intractable in the evening simply dissolve overnight; the morning light brings clarity, and the solution seems obvious.

Another invaluable technique, when faced with a problem or idea or opportunity, is to list all the pros and cons. This might seem obvious, but it's effective. If the scale tips in favor of one side right away, your decision is easy. If the pros and cons balance out, let your subconscious deal with it. It will find the right answer.

One point: If the pros and cons balance out evenly, this can indicate that the plan will run up against problems. Doubt can eventually undermine your enthusiasm and your belief in yourself. If you only half-believe in a project, the results will match the expectations.

THE IDEAL TIME IS NOW

Most people make the mistake of waiting for the ideal time. This is just another excuse. The ideal time to start succeeding is today, this very minute. Write down a plan of what you want to achieve, make that phone call you've been thinking of, or write that letter you've been intending to write. Do it now.

The fundamental weakness that ruins so many

people's lives is procrastination. Time is a vital component of any dream. An idea that might be a brilliant success today might completely fail in a year. A phone call might work wonders at one moment and come to absolutely nothing at all at another. The best decision, almost always, is to *do it now*.

All successful people have developed the ability to make decisions and act quickly on those decisions. "Haste hinders good counsel" — so the proverb goes. Yet procrastination and slowness surely do more wrong than hasty decisions.

STICK TO YOUR DECISION

Another characteristic of successful people is that they stick to their decisions, regardless of circumstances, past failures, temporary setbacks, or others' opinions.

Sticking to your final decision confirms your inner certainty that you have aimed correctly. Those who constantly change their minds will never be successful. Vacillation is a sign of a mental state dominated by doubt. Since you have seen that circumstances reflect your inner thoughts, there can be no question that doubt leads straight to failure. Consequently, success depends on two vital factors: (1) Making clear decisions, and (2) sticking to them while jumping straight into action.

You need to stick to your decisions, yet you also need to know when to let them go. This is not a contradiction. In both cases, when you rely on your intuition, you'll receive the guidance you need. Even the most astute entrepreneurs have made decisions that took them to places they didn't anticipate. It's vital, therefore, not to be overly rigid. One key to success is finding the delicate balance between persistence and flexibility.

DON'T GIVE UP TOO QUICKLY

Most people fail because they give up *much* too quickly. They throw in the towel after one or two failures. Pride or a lack of self-confidence makes people give up too quickly. Colonel Sanders tried dozens of different times to sell his chicken before he finally succeeded. An engineer at Head, a sporting goods company, performed forty-three tests before he successfully developed a metal ski. If he had given up after a dozen attempts, or even forty-two attempts, someone else would have invented it.

All great success stories are punctuated with failures. Positive people don't let themselves be beaten down by their first blunders. And we all make blunders at first, until we figure out what works.

Many successful people look at it in a way that

recognizes a somewhat mysterious phenomenon: Life seems to have been designed as some sort of test. When people show they can overcome obstacles and failures with unswerving persistence and faith, life seems to lay down its weapons of opposition, and fame and fortune appear, as if charmed by their vision and strength. Success often follows a resounding failure, as if life wants to reward the brave soul able to surmount such a devastating setback.

The most successful people, almost without exception, all failed — often more than once — before they were successful. But they didn't give up. They tried and tried again.

LEARN FROM PAST MISTAKES

There is no shame in making a mistake — though it's generally a waste of time and energy to make the same mistake twice. If we thoughtfully examine why we failed, we gain a clearer understanding of how to succeed. In this way, each failure leads us closer to success.

Determination, a quality absent in most people, is almost always generously rewarded. It must not, however, be confused with blind pigheadedness. To adapt quickly is one of the keys to success; so is pragmatic trial and error. Rely on your intuition, take action, and keep going.

Soichiro Honda, chairman of Honda, makes an important point:

> When days become this dark and gloomy, it means that the treasure I am looking for is about to be discovered. The great flash of light and hope that bursts forth makes me instantly forget my long hours of tedious work.

Once we achieve success, we see that all our past mistakes were an essential part of our ongoing education. We never regret the past: Every failure we created has served us well, for our success is built on the understanding we gained from all our past mistakes and missteps.

❧ SUMMARY AND RECOMMENDED ACTION ❧

1. *What do you want?* State it simply, and present a clear request to your subconscious mind. Write it out. Repeat it to yourself, preferably at night before going to bed. Your subconscious will demonstrate its limitless power and guide you to the people, places, and circumstances that will lead you to fulfillment of your dreams.

2. *Look for possibilities where others see only difficulties or impossibilities.* Look for the opportunity within every adversity. If you believe that every time a difficult situation occurs you're being shown something, and you're learning something, you will make rapid progress on your journey to success.

3. *Remember to trust your intuition.* An important step in learning to hear and follow your intuition is simply to practice "checking in" regularly — at least twice a day. Take a moment or two to relax and tune in to your gut feelings. Ask for help and guidance when you need it, and listen for answers, which may come in many forms: words, images, or feelings, from within you, or from your world.

Chapter Five

DO WHAT YOU LOVE

I believe if you have talent and skill,
you should spin off on your own
and become captain of your own destiny.

— GEORGE LUCAS, FILMMAKER AND FOUNDER
AND CHAIRMAN OF LUCAS ARTS

I would love to set up my own business, but I
don't have the ability or financing."

"My dream was to become an actor, but my
parents laughed at the idea. I work for the govern-
ment instead."

"My job bores me to tears, but there's so much
unemployment and downsizing going on that I'd
better not kid myself about finding a better one."

"I used to dream of being a lawyer, but it would take years."

How often have we heard words like these, or variations on the same themes? How often have you had similar thoughts? Out of every ten people, how many can boast of really enjoying their jobs? Unfortunately, most people simply don't like what they do for a living. They're convinced that they're stuck in their drudgery, that they will never be able to change their situations. Fate, in other words, has permanently sentenced them to a life of mediocrity.

If you dislike your job, consider the following: You could die without having done what you really want to do. Aren't you worth more than that?

Take a typical day in the life of so many people: They work eight hours at a job they don't particularly enjoy, and then sleep eight hours. This leaves them with eight hours they typically use to recover and to try to forget the frustrations heaped on them during the day. Their dissatisfaction affects their relationships with their spouses, children, and friends. And yet, they continue, *believing they must*.

Most people unwillingly drag themselves to work on Monday morning and watch the clock until Friday afternoon, when they can finally throw off the shackles they had to endure for five long, painful days. They only really live for two out of seven days, with Saturday generally spent winding down or getting life's necessities together, and Sunday already haunted by the gloomy specter of Monday-morning blues. And they tolerate this, year after year.

This passive, fatalistic view of life can be changed. Nothing obliges you to keep working at a job you don't like. You can do something about it. An inspiring job exists to fulfill everyone's passion. And you could start it right now. Is life so poorly designed that it's meant to frustrate us constantly and deprive us of what we truly want? Life isn't that cruel. At least, it doesn't have to be. *It's your choice*.

LIFE GIVES US EXACTLY WHAT WE EXPECT

The belief that dreams are impossible to achieve prevents most people from getting what they want. Their experience certainly seems to support this belief. They get exactly what they expect from life: boredom, frustration, obstacles, and small incomes. People are what they believe themselves to be, no more, no less.

Denying your personal inclinations and ambitions normally begins very early in life. Yet, to be happy and fulfilled, we have to be courageous enough to be ourselves, to discover what we want, and to go after it. We have to stop denying ourselves because of fear, doubt, or conformity to some "normal" behavior or way of life. It's a fallacy that we have to do unfulfilling things to earn a living.

In fact, to be successful, you have to first do what you enjoy in life. If you don't enjoy your work, you can't do it well. This is an absolute principle. When your heart isn't in something, you experience a drastic slump in energy and motivation. You inevitably come up with mediocre results, or at least with a much poorer performance than you would if you loved what you were doing. It then follows that your boss, associates, clients, or customers can't be completely satisfied with what you have accomplished.

As an unhappy employee, chances are slim that you will get promoted to a more interesting position or receive a substantial raise. As an unhappy business owner, chances are small that your business will flourish. Since you rarely work alone, your unhappiness can drag your colleagues down. The monetary rewards you get will reflect this. And with poor monetary compensation, your motivation and the quality of your work plummets — another vicious cycle!

Mark McCormack, author of *What They Don't Teach You at Harvard Business School*, makes this excellent point:

> Boredom occurs when the learning curve flattens out. It can happen to anyone at any

level of the corporation. In fact, it occurs most often in successful people who need more challenge and stimulation than do others. If you're bored it's your fault. You just aren't working hard enough at making your job interesting. It is also probably the reason you haven't been offered anything better. Find out what you love to do and you will be successful at it.

DO WHAT YOU LOVE

When we say — emphatically — that you must love your work, we are in no way suggesting that an ideal job will be devoid of frustration, disappointment, and problems. Every successful person has faced periods of discouragement, frustration, and even self-doubt. Your dream job will not be heaven on earth every day. It's more like true love: The deep bonds that bring and keep two people together allow them to overcome the dilemmas and obstacles that appear along the way. Thomas Watson, founder of IBM, said it this way: "Make room in your heart for work and put some heart into your work."

Successful people are ruled by passion and their hearts. They are romantics, whether in art or in the world of business. They are spurred into action by their love of their work and their desire to do new things, to take up new challenges, to face new risks. They carry their dreams in their hearts — and they do everything they can to achieve them.

PASSION AND POWER

In *Work with Passion*, author Nancy Anderson defines passion:

> Passion is intense emotional excitement. It is a feeling that comes to those who feel intensely about some object, person, ideal, or belief. Human passions are released to create both good and evil. There are many examples in history that show the difference one passionate person can make. Every love story, every major change in history — social, economic, philosophical, and artistic — came about because of the participation of *passionate* individuals.
>
> We all have the capacity to feel intense emotional excitement. However, few of us *act* on our passions. We bury our passion because, among other reasons, we were ridiculed early in life because our enthusiasm was not backed up with expertise. As soon as you give yourself permission to feel

whatever you feel, that power will resurface, surprising all who "knew you when." Then you will take action on those feelings.

Power is *the ability to take action*. As an adult, you know that your decisions are your choices. It is no longer necessary to do anything you hate — you can choose to do only what you truly love to do. That is power. That is passion in action.

Here's a good question to ask yourself: If you won ten million dollars, would you stay in your present job? If your answer is "yes," congratulations! If not, then creating a situation in which you would answer "yes" to that question could be a very important goal. Here are a few principles to move you toward this goal:

- The only way to be happy and successful is to do what you truly enjoy doing. There is an ideal job or career for each one of us, a service that we can provide that no one else can do in quite the same way.

- You can do whatever you like, provided you put the necessary energy and determination into it.

- You alone can shape your destiny and decide to do what you enjoy, regardless of obstacles. The greatest barrier to success is yourself.

- Dare to do what you love. Overcome your fear-based mental and emotional blocks and you will succeed.

William O'Brian of Hanover Insurance puts it this way in an interview with Peter Senge in *The Fifth Discipline*: "To seek personal fulfillment only outside of work and to ignore the significant portion of our lives that we spend working would be to limit our opportunities to be happy and complete human beings."

BECOME THE BEST AT WHAT YOU DO

In his autobiography, Henry Ford said, "I determined absolutely that never would I join a company in which finance came before the work." For Ford, "the only foundation of real business is service."

Success is built on service. Successful service is built on one attitude: the attitude of doing the best we can, working to be the best in our field. Many successful people are motivated into action by the need to do things well and to accomplish something that will help other people. Making a profit is not their primary purpose, yet they usually make far more money than those who work primarily for profit. Steve Jobs, founder of Apple Computer, has said, "We're doing this because we really care about the higher educational process, not because we want to make a buck."

Wealth is the reward we receive in exchange for services we render. If we give the best service, then we can expect a commensurate reward. It is very powerful, then, to program our subconscious toward becoming the best in our field in a given period of time. As we give ourselves completely to our gift — our service — our gift gives back to us abundantly.

BECOME AN EXPERT IN YOUR CHOSEN FIELD

While you don't necessarily have to pursue years of formal education, it's invaluable to pursue all avenues to becoming an expert in your field.

In the world today, when last month's computer system is already out of date, you have to keep up with change. One of the fundamentals of success is having in-depth knowledge or specialization in your work. A lack of knowledge is one of the major roadblocks to success.

Start by considering the products or services

you have to offer to the public before looking for profits. With a good product or service, money comes naturally. When you become the best in your field, and focus on serving, the money will follow. This is an ancient law that never fails.

BE AN ORIGINAL

Formal education is certainly not sufficient to guarantee success. Something more is needed — a spark of originality or boldness, which schools often fail to teach and sometimes stifle altogether. All too often, schools level out the thinking process and suppress the creativity that allows you to see new possibilities and original solutions.

Education, and society in general, too often nip personal aspirations in the bud. This insidious process begins early in life. Our fears of being different and our need to conform support the part of our subconscious programming that limits our dreams, ideas, and aspirations.

We all naturally imitate those around us, especially when we're young. Unfortunately, the vast majority of people have imitated passionless jobs, financial struggle, and mediocrity.

A small, inner voice nevertheless survives within each of us. Timid and worried, it whispers to us that our public images are false, that our genuine personalities are hidden and unexpressed. Frustration, sadness, and, in some cases, a dead feeling inside are some of the burdens we heap upon ourselves when we deny who we are and what we have to offer.

If we want to succeed, we have to be different. We have to fully be ourselves and not be afraid to assert our true personalities. We are unique individuals with a unique purpose in life. Each of us is an original.

MAKE YOUR DESIRES INTO INTENTIONS, AND MAKE THEM CRYSTAL CLEAR

"I don't have the faintest idea what I really want to do...." Sound familiar? This is an all-too-common complaint. So many people are overwhelmed with confusion, and yet they never sit down and ask themselves the simplest questions — the kind of questions we ask throughout this book. The answers to these questions would dissolve their confusion in an instant. When people complain about not knowing what they want to do with their lives, it's obvious they have spent years stifling their aspirations and ignoring their inner selves. By conforming to other people's expectations and ways of life, they have forgotten who they are and have sowed the seeds of their confusion.

Anyone who doesn't really know what he or she wants to do and doesn't establish clear-cut goals will find it hard to succeed. The opposite is also true: *When we know perfectly well what we want to do in life, when our desire is crystal clear, the conditions enabling us to achieve it soon appear.* Often, extremely precise desires are fulfilled almost immediately.

A perfectly straightforward desire — devoid of hesitation, ambiguity, and contradiction — is very rare indeed. Vague, confused ambitions create a muddled subconscious. Since our aspirations are unclear, the results will be nebulous. A metamorphosis has to take place *within* — we have to form a clear picture of our ambitions and desires. We have to sculpt them to be clear and precise.

Don't underestimate the importance of this inner change. Until we are sure what we want, we won't get it. All successful people have unmistakable, clear ambitions and intentions. Their career choices were spawned by a deep sense of intuition that left no room for doubt. One of the most powerful keys to success, therefore, is knowing exactly what you want to be, do, and have.

Deepak Chopra's words are worth repeating here: "Inherent in every intention and desire is the mechanics for its fulfillment." In *The Seven Spiritual Laws of Success*, Chopra illuminates intention and desire in more detail, and adds another very important element of true, lasting success: *detachment*.

> Intention lays the groundwork for the effortless, spontaneous, frictionless flow of pure potentiality seeking expression from the unmanifest to the manifest. . . .
>
> Intention is the real power behind desire. Intent alone is very powerful, because intent is desire without attachment to the outcome. Desire alone is weak, because desire in most people is intention with attachment. . . . Intention combined with detachment leads to life-centered, present-moment awareness. And when action is performed in present-moment awareness, it is most effective. Your intent is for the future, but your attention is in the present. As long as your attention is in the present, then your intent for the future will manifest, because the future is created in the present. Accept the present and intend the future. The future is something you can always create through detached intention.

Turn your wishes into crystal-clear *desires*. Turn your desires into *intentions*. Once you intend to do something, 90 percent of your perceived obstacles vanish — and you have the tools to overcome the remaining 10 percent. Such is the power of your intent!

When you make an absolutely clear intention to do something, and yet are not attached to the results, you have an infallible formula for success and fulfillment.

❧ SUMMARY AND RECOMMENDED ACTION ❧

To integrate passion and power in your work life and to become the best at what you do:

1. *Think about your life as it is; then picture how you want it to be.* If you're not doing what you like, make a list of all of the reasons you can think of that support your belief that you can't do what truly excites and pleases you. Now go over the list point by point and think about each reason. Are these obstacles really valid? If you can understand the principles in this book, you will understand that every obstacle can be overcome and turned into an opportunity. As Henry Ford said, "Whether you think you can or you think you can't, you're right."

2. *Ask yourself, if you had all the time and money in the world, what would you do?* If you would still do what you currently do, then you are on the right track, because you are passionate about what you do. If you would rather be doing something else, ask yourself: In what ways can I do the things I want now? How can I begin to live the life I want to live ideally?

3. *Become aware of your inner dialogue, as often as you possibly can.* Life gives you exactly what you expect. You write your own script in the drama of life, with every word you think and say — so it's up to you to write a better script for yourself.

4. *In a relaxed state, repeat the following affirmations, or formulas for success, to yourself:*

- I am unique. I have something to offer.

- It is my right and duty to be myself.

- I am becoming successful. I invite success and prosperity into my life.

- I attract the people and situations that will help me offer my service.

- Every day, in every way, I am getting better and better.

5. *At night, ask your subconscious to help you discover how you can be a complete success, make all the money you want, and serve humanity and the earth.* Fall asleep knowing that the answer already lies within you, and that you have already obtained what you asked for. The formidable power of your subconscious will work continuously, night and day, as long as you have steered it in the right direction.

Chapter Six

THE MAGIC OF GOALS

*I resolved first to make enough money so
I'd never be stopped from finishing anything.*
— WILLIAM P. LEAR, LEAR JET INC.

Once we have discovered our passion, the field in which we want to succeed, we can concentrate on fulfilling our plans. Some of the best plans are the simplest. Thomas Peters and Robert Waterman's *In Search of Excellence* discusses the paradox of simplicity:

> Many of today's managers — MBA-trained and the like — may be a little bit too smart

for their own good. The smart ones are the ones who shift direction all the time, based upon the latest output from the expected value equation. The ones who juggle hundred-variable models with facility; the ones who design complicated incentive systems; the ones who wire up matrix structures; the ones who have 200-page strategic plans and 500-page market requirement documents that are but step one in product development exercises.

Our "dumber" friends are different. They just don't understand why every customer can't have personalized service, even in the potato chip business. They are personally affronted . . . when a bottle of beer goes sour. They can't understand why a regular flow of new products isn't possible, or why a worker can't contribute a suggestion every couple of weeks. Simpleminded fellows, really; simplistic even. Yes, simplistic has a negative connotation. But the people who lead the excellent companies are a bit simplistic.

To believe that we can make as much money as we want, to believe in our dreams, to disregard negative people, we need a good dose of naivete and simplicity. People who are too rational or intelligent can succeed, but their intelligence can limit the degree of their success if it limits in any way the vast field of their dreams.

MAKE ONE CLEAR GOAL

People who don't succeed don't have precise goals. Any objectives they do have are, on some deep level, invariably low. They succeed at mediocrity or failure.

Some people don't even begin to set goals because of the overwhelmingly negative conversations they carry on in their subconscious. Almost all successful people started achieving their dreams only when they set clear goals and timelines for meeting them. (There may be some people who are exceptions to this rule — but we don't know of any.)

Set a precise goal, with a precise amount of income, and a time plan to make it. You'll discover that this is an important difference between those who succeed and those who don't. *We achieve what we plan to achieve, no more, no less.*

There is a story often repeated in business books about the salesman who could never sell more than

$25,000 worth of his product in a month. He was assigned to a territory where average sales were well below that amount, and he managed to sell $25,000 a month — quite an achievement for that territory. His manager sent him to a larger area where other salespeople were performing much better than that. His result: $25,000 a month. The dilemma he faced was clearly based on his goals and self-image. He didn't believe he could sell more (or less) than $25,000 a month, and his subconscious was set accordingly. This story is a good example of the power of the subconscious and the fact that we achieve any objective our subconscious sets for us.

Haven't your own experiences been directly linked to your objectives? Anyone with a vague, uncertain target — or no target at all — will get vague results, or no results at all. On the other hand, anyone who establishes a specific goal, backed with a specific plan of action, achieves it.

Why is this? The answer is within our subconscious mind: A clear target is the most simple and effective way of programming your subconscious. You won't necessarily have to work harder to achieve this goal; you might even have to work less. In the past, success has often been equated with long hours of hard work. But you'll soon find that when you align yourself with your purpose, release negativity, and program yourself for reaching your goals, you achieve results with less effort. It is possible to work less and get better results. A great many people know this is true. The secret lies in making a clear goal.

Even among the hardworking and success-oriented, a great many people don't have a specific objective in mind. Many people are satisfied with a slight improvement in their lives without ever considering or daring to set themselves a clear-cut figure that represents a *substantial* improvement in their lives, something that moves them toward the kind of life they *ideally* want to live.

What is your goal for next year? How much do you want to earn? $50,000? $100,000? $500,000? A million dollars? If you want your lifestyle to improve substantially — a perfectly legitimate desire — ask yourself what goal you have to set. If you want a brighter future, establish your goals and determine how much time and energy you are willing and able to channel into reaching them. If all you can do is dream of getting a promotion or a fantastic job offer, but you don't have a specific objective, the "miracle" you are expecting will not happen. Your self-worth is exactly what you think it is.

Every successful person realizes this is an obvious truth: If you make a clear goal and begin to take the next apparent steps toward its realization — whatever steps are required to convince your subconscious you are serious about focusing on that goal — you will soon find you have reached it.

YOU ARE WORTH MUCH MORE THAN YOU BELIEVE

The greatest limitations people impose on themselves are created in their own minds. A person's worth is exactly what he or she believes it to be, no more, no less. Most people underestimate themselves, even if they appear self-confident. Those who know, deep down, that they are truly valuable are few and far between. Almost everyone has some degree of an inferiority complex, and this causes them to believe they are unworthy of success, of other people's esteem, or of much money.

The best way to increase your worth is to build your self-esteem. We have already presented techniques useful for bringing about fundamental change. One of the best ways of accomplishing this is to work with a specific monetary objective.

SETTING YOURSELF AN EXACT OBJECTIVE IS TRULY MAGICAL

Usually the first time you set yourself a specific monetary goal, you retain a certain amount of skepticism that limits the clarity and power of your ambition. So, make your first goals realistic; then, when you achieve your first goal, you can set yourself an even higher goal. Make this goal more of a *stretch*. Those who set themselves a clear target for the first time are generally surprised when they reach it and often go beyond it!

Challenge yourself to reach your goal. It's an exciting game that brings rewarding dividends. Perhaps you'll reach your goal in six months instead of the year you initially gave yourself. We've seen this happen many times. Setting yourself an exact objective is truly magical.

YOU ARE WORTH INFINITELY MORE THAN YOU BELIEVE

It's not an exaggeration — it's the truth: You are worth *infinitely* more than you believe. The only problem is, quite possibly, no one has ever told you that before. Some people have probably tried their best to persuade you that the opposite is true.

Intelligence, work, motivation, imagination, discipline, and experience are, of course, important ingredients for success — but how many people do you know who have these qualities but still don't succeed, or don't live up to their full potential? Perhaps the same is true for you. Despite your obvious talents and efforts, success inexplicably escapes you. You meet people at work or at other companies who don't appear to be any more specially gifted than you, but yet they get the raise, the promotion, and achieve an enviable level of success. Keep this in mind: *Their self-images have determined their goals, which have determined their lifestyles.* And your self-image has determined your goals, which have determined your lifestyle.

Overcome your mental limitations and increase your self-worth by aiming as high as possible. It's not any harder for your subconscious to help you reach a higher objective than a lower one. And it's certainly much more enjoyable!

Make your goal a magnificent obsession. Write it down in several places to keep it well in sight. Above all, keep it constantly in mind. A major principle ruling the mind is that *energy goes wherever your thoughts go.* By repeatedly thinking of your goal and making it a fixed idea, all your energy channels itself into helping you be successful. And thanks to the continuous work of your subconscious, circumstances and people will help you reach your goal in new and surprising ways.

MAKE YOUR GOAL A SINGLE, FIXED IDEA

A goal is like a magnifying glass: As a magnifying glass can focus the sun's energy to ignite a fire, a goal focuses your energy to make your objective a reality. Make your primary goal into a single, simple, fixed idea. This fixed idea not only allows you to increase your energy and level of success but also prevents a very serious mistake — scattering your energy. A fixed goal inevitably leads you to success.

The single-mindedness of a fixed idea also enables you to direct your professional and personal life more clearly, and with less effort. Everything that brings you closer to your goal should be encouraged. And you should let go of everything that distances you from it. How can you tell if something is bringing you closer or not? Your intuition will tell you in its usual way: a subtle feeling, a comment from a friend or partner, a phrase in a book or an article that resonates with truth for you.

Ask yourself for guidance, and you'll receive it. Create clear goals, and you'll achieve them.

❧ **SUMMARY AND RECOMMENDED ACTION** ❧

1. *Take a piece of paper and write down how much you'd like to earn next year.* When you have finished, consider this: When you created your goal, you based it on your self-image. Did you write down $40,000? If you did, that's what you thought you were worth. And you're right: You are worth exactly what you think you're worth. And when you can say $80,000, or $200,000, or a million, that's what you'll be worth. *You are worth what you believe you are worth.* And yet, your subconscious is unlimited, and so your potential is unlimited. It's true, therefore, that you are worth much more than you currently believe.

2. *Double the amount you wrote down a moment ago.* Assess your reaction. If you initially wrote down $50,000, why didn't you begin with $100,000? How do you feel about this larger goal? Do you think it's completely far-fetched? Do you think that $100,000 is a lot? Too much? Many people would disagree with you. Each year, thousands of people become

millionaires, and *millions* of people have yearly incomes far in excess of $100,000. They had enough of a positive self-image to aim for this income, and to go after it.

3. *In spite of what we've just said, don't set an overly unrealistic goal for yourself for your first year.* Do it step by step, but eventually make it ambitious. If you aim high and almost make it, you'll still have achieved a satisfying result. But if your target is low and you barely make it, you'll be disappointed and will have made very little progress. Set a goal that stretches you and challenges your subconscious, but don't make it so high that it feels completely unachievable. Even though the goal-setting process is concrete and rational, the most important thing is convincing your subconscious that you're ready for this goal. You'll know it when you're ready. It will feel right; it will feel like a challenge you can't wait to take. Then the world will give you exactly what you ask for — no more, no less.

Chapter Seven

A PLAN OF ACTION

*I believe the decision to focus your efforts is
extremely important, not only in the early days of
a company but later on as well.*
— DAVID PACKARD, HEWLETT-PACKARD

The most vital step on your path to success is preparing a step-by-step plan of action so that your intention becomes solidified, consciously and subconsciously. What actually unfolds may be quite different from your step-by-step plan — in fact, it *probably* will be quite different — but you'll reach the goal, nonetheless, soon after your intention is solid and unwavering.

Some jobs, unfortunately, will never bring great financial rewards; if money simply doesn't matter to you, so much the better. But if you want financial security and the means to pursue your dreams, change jobs, if necessary. Look for a position in a field that is compatible with your passion, talents, and skills, and offers a good salary as well. Or start your own business — in your spare time, if necessary.

No human being is infallible, not even the most experienced businessperson. Only those who do nothing never make mistakes. Even if you undergo temporary setbacks, you will still achieve your goals, provided your subconscious is properly programmed. This is the power of a precise monetary goal and a plan of action with a deadline.

PREPARE A STEP-BY-STEP PLAN OF ACTION TO SOLIDIFY YOUR INTENTIONS

A step-by-step plan of action convinces your subconscious that your desire, your dream, your wishful thinking has become an *intention*. You intend to accomplish this goal and create this situation in your life. The proof of your intention is your step-by-step plan. Convinced, your unlimited subconscious goes to work. You create exactly what you intend to create — no more, no less.

Applying your plan of action can mean taking risks that cause significant personal insecurity, especially if it's the first time you have set a goal and established a clear plan of action. Almost any change — even a change for the better — generates a certain amount of anxiety. Most people's need for security is so great that they are prepared to sacrifice their most precious dreams for it. Don't be afraid to forge ahead. You'll never regret it. We don't know of anyone who ever regretted taking a risk, when it was a step toward realizing a dream.

We recommend that you not set more than two separate goals in one area of your life at a time. Pursuing too many goals at once diffuses your concentration and makes your work less effective. Pursuing goals in different areas of your life simultaneously, however, such as career, home, fitness, improved relationships, or finishing the next draft of your thesis or book is advantageous; each improvement benefits the other areas of your life.

Another highly beneficial action is to set goals for your future: one year, five years, ten, twenty-five, even fifty years into the future. Where do you want to be when you are sixty? What kind of person would you like to be when you are eighty? What kind of life are you dreaming of? How about your health and fitness? Do you want to have children? What do you want to have accomplished?

Don't limit yourself. Sit down and prepare a step-by-step plan.

We know many people who have written out a step-by-step plan for something, put it away somewhere and forgotten about it, and then discovered later they had fulfilled their plan, without even consciously thinking about it! We don't recommend this, of course — we recommend a healthy amount of repetition of your goals — but we have seen it happen many times.

YOU ARE THE ARCHITECT OF YOUR LIFE — HOW WOULD YOU LIKE TO CREATE IT?

Disregard your present situation, your previous failures, your past. Forget about your age, as well. Many people well into their sixties and seventies know the best is yet to come. We can make our lives rich and full at any age. Often the dreams we nourish come true more easily than we expect — regardless of our age or current situation.

When you can picture yourself in an ideal future, when you know what you would like to do for the rest of your life, your short-term goals become far more clear and meaningful. You have a reason to get out of bed every morning and take steps that bring you closer to fulfillment.

You have charted the course of your life. You have become a visionary.

Picturing your life in this way — imagining your ideal scene — can literally shape your future, because through positive dreaming, through creative visualization, you program your subconscious. You flood it with images that are likely to come true. You hold the reins of command. You are indeed the architect of your life. Your blueprints are your goals and your ideal scene of your life in the future.

Your long-term goals not only define your ideal in life, they help to *create* it. They simplify many choices that would otherwise seem difficult or, worse still, arbitrary or absurd. When you don't know what you want to do with your life, it's difficult sometimes to make even the most insignificant day-to-day decisions. They don't seem part of a greater plan that gives meaning to your thoughts and actions.

Making a life plan is stimulating and motivating, and it contributes to success in all areas of life. Keep in mind, however, the need to remain flexible regarding the future, since life involves constant adaptation. What you are doing in five or ten years may not necessarily be what you expect — it might be much better than you ever dreamed possible.

When our minds are well programmed, the situations that develop are always better than our previous situations. Every day, in every way, we get better and better. As we develop, our full potential becomes more and more realized, and the plans we dream up are bolder, more ambitious, more expansive. We often drop some of our initial plans along the way, usually because we were "thinking too small." As our self-image expands, our success in the world expands as well. We end up constantly progressing toward greater self-fulfillment — and personal enrichment, if that's one of our goals.

Now carefully plan your main objective for the next year — while still remaining flexible enough to respond to unforeseen opportunities that may very well come up. You'll have a clear picture of the work and effort you must put in to reach your goal. Divide your yearly goal into months, and then into weeks. Sound planning prevents a lot of worry and delay, and it keeps you moving forward toward your goal.

CHARACTER EQUALS DESTINY

It is all well and good to set an objective — it is necessary for anyone wishing to be successful — but to try to work toward it day by day requires discipline. And the best discipline is the one we, and no one else, impose on ourselves. The Greek philosopher Heraclitus said, "Character equals destiny." If we look around at all the people we know, we see there are no exceptions to this rule. All successful women and men have strong character and are highly disciplined, each in their own way. No one succeeds without strength of character. To become our own master and take our destiny in hand, we need discipline.

By discipline, we don't mean a rigid schedule that excludes fantasy and relaxation. And we certainly don't mean workaholism. Discipline also means allowing enough time to rest, exercise, and properly nourish our bodies, enough time to meet family commitments, enough time for fun, enough time to be alone.

Overwork is never productive. Complaining of overwork is fashionable these days — and since most people don't use a tenth of their potential, they are overworked but never seem to accomplish much. They work too hard, and still lack discipline. They haven't created the habits that lead to success.

SUCCESS IS A HABIT

Discipline and positive mental programming lead naturally to developing our own methods and ways of organization, discovering our personal working rhythm and patterns, and creating the habit of success. Until now, failure or mediocrity has simply been a habit. By replacing one habit with another, our new habit becomes second nature. Success is then irresistibly attracted to us.

As the old saying goes: "Sow a thought, and you reap an action; sow an action, and you reap a habit; sow a habit, and you reap a character; sow a character, and you reap a destiny." These are words that have the power to change the course of our lives.

❧ SUMMARY AND RECOMMENDED ACTION ❧

1. *Take a piece of paper and write down what you would like to do with your life*. Add as many details as possible. What kind of work would you like to do? How much money would you like to earn? In five years? In ten years? In twenty-five years? What kind of house would you like to live in? What kind of friends would you like to have? Will traveling be part of your life? Where will you spend your vacations? What about your family life? Write all of this down in as much detail as possible.

2. *Identify next year's objective*. Once you have your goal clearly in mind for the

year to come, make a step-by-step plan to achieve it. Write down, in order, the things you need to accomplish. Set a date for each stage, and keep your deadlines in mind. And prepare yourself for some truly miraculous results.

Conclusion

Nothing in the world can take the place of persistence.
Talent will not: nothing is more common than
unsuccessful people with talent.
Genius will not: unrewarded genius is almost a proverb.
Education will not: the world is full of educated derelicts.
Persistence and determination alone are omnipotent.

— THOMAS WATSON, FOUNDER OF IBM

There are no "secrets of success." Almost all successful people enjoy sharing what they have learned along the way with those who are interested. We've certainly enjoyed writing this book, and telling you, as clearly as we can, not the secrets but the techniques, the practices, the knowledge, and the truths that have been instrumental to our success. The book is brief, but don't let that fool you: It doesn't take volumes to explain the powerful principles of success.

We can summarize them even more briefly:

- Imagine the life you want, and decide — make an intention — to go for it.

- Discover what you love and make it your vocation. *Vocation* comes from the Latin *vocare*, "to call." Find your calling.

- Devote your energy, your lifeblood, to your calling; the joy and fulfillment you receive generate even more energy.

- Know what you want; set clear goals with time plans for their completion. Turn your desires into intentions, and take the first steps toward achieving your intentions.

- Discover how to combine a clear intention — a single, focused objective — with nonattachment. Let your success unfold and grow with its own rhythm, in its own time. Have clear goals, yet don't become attached to results. Have clear objectives for the future, but live fully in the present, enjoying the present moment.

- Turn obstacles and past failures into an impetus for success. Your failures have given you the education you need to create abundant success in your life.

- Become an expert in your field. Always improve your skills and knowledge. Education is endless.

- See possibilities where others see only problems or impossibilities. Stretch your imagination. The world is full of infinite possibilities!

- Discover your own comfortable, natural working rhythm, your own form of discipline.

- Be persistent. The only real failure is giving up.

- Give back and give thanks. Give away at least 10 percent of your income — and eventually much more, as you become more and more successful. The more you give, the more you will receive. This is an infallible truth. You have the power to create a lot of good in the world for a lot of people.

- Live the life you want. Now. Keep reminding yourself that every day in every way, your life is getting better and better.

Eileen Caddy, cofounder of the Findhorn community in Scotland, said it beautifully: "The secret of making something work in your lives is, first of all, the deep desire to make it work, then the faith and belief that it can work, then to hold that clear, definite vision in your consciousness and see it working out."

You have all the tools. Now it's up to you to use them.

References

CHAPTER 1. WHERE DO I START?

Allen, Marc. *Visionary Business: An Entrepreneur's Guide to Success*. Novato, CA: New World Library, 1995.

Inamori, Kazuo. *A Passion for Success: Practical, Inspirational, and Spiritual Insight from Japan's Leading Entrepreneur*. New York: McGraw-Hill, 1995.

Allen, James. *As You Think*. Edited by Marc Allen. Novato, CA: New World Library, 1998.

CHAPTER 2. WEALTH IS A STATE OF MIND

Senge, Peter M. *The Fifth Discipline: The Art & Practice of the Learning Organization*. New York: Doubleday, 1990.

Peters, Thomas, and Robert Waterman. *In Search of Excellence: Lessons from America's Best-Run Companies*. New York: Harper & Row, 1982.

Gawain, Shakti. *Creative Visualization*. Novato, CA: New World Library, 2002.

CHAPTER 3. ELIMINATING MENTAL BLOCKS

Harman, Willis. *Global Mind Change: The Promise of the Twenty-first Century*. 2nd ed. Sausalito, CA: Institute of Noetic Sciences / Berrett-Koehler Publishers, 1998.

Chopra, Deepak. *The Seven Spiritual Laws of Success*. Novato, CA: Amber-Allen Publishing / New World Library, 1994.

Covey, Stephen R. *The Seven Habits of Highly Effective People: Powerful Lessons in Personal Change*. New York: Free Press, 1990.

CHAPTER 4. MAKING DECISIONS

McCormack, Mark. *What They Don't Teach You at Harvard Business School*. New York: Bantam, 1986.

Walton, Sam. *Sam Walton — Made in America:*

My Story. With John Huey. New York: Bantam, 1993.

Gawain, Shakti. *Living in the Light: A Guide to Personal and Planetary Transformation*. With Laurel King. Novato, CA: Nataraj Publishing, 1998.

CHAPTER 5. DO WHAT YOU LOVE

McCormack, Mark. *What They Don't Teach You at Harvard Business School*. New York: Bantam, 1986.

Anderson, Nancy. *Work with Passion: How to Do What You Love for a Living*. Novato, CA: New World Library, 1995.

Senge, Peter M. *The Fifth Discipline: The Art & Practice of the Learning Organization*. New York: Doubleday, 1990.

Henry Ford, *My Life and Work — An Autobiography of Henry Ford*. Sioux Falls, SD: NuVision Publications, 2007.

Chopra, Deepak. *The Seven Spiritual Laws of Success*. Novato, CA: Amber-Allen Publishing / New World Library, 1994.

CHAPTER 6. THE MAGIC OF GOALS

Peters, Thomas, and Robert Waterman. *In Search of Excellence: Lessons from America's Best-Run Companies*. New York: Harper & Row, 1982.

About the Authors

Mark Fisher told a fictionalized story of his life in his first book, *The Instant Millionaire*. By studying with a mentor, he learned the principles of success he writes about in both that book and this one. He has interests in publishing and real estate and lives in Montreal, Canada.

The day he turned thirty, Marc Allen cofounded New World Library with Shakti Gawain. He has written numerous books, including *Visionary Business*, *A Visionary Life*, *The Millionaire Course*, and *The Type-Z Guide to Success*. He has also recorded several albums of music, including *Awakening*, *Breathe*, and *Solo Flight*. He is a popular speaker and seminar leader based in the San Francisco Bay Area. For more about Marc, see www.MarcAllen.com. For more about his music, see www.Watercourse Media.com. For more about New World Library, see www.NewWorldLibrary.com.